FISHING

is for me

FISHING
is for me

text and photographs by
Art Thomas

 Lerner Publications Company   Minneapolis

The author wishes to thank Kevin Wiseman and Virgil Rosario and their families, Anthony Thomas, Carl Badger, and the Hinkley Lake boat dock staff.

Photographs on pages 41, 42, 43, and 44 courtesy of Minnesota Department of Natural Resources

To the memory of my mother, Anne Thomas

LIBRARY OF CONGRESS CATALOGING IN PUBLICATION DATA

Thomas, Art, 1952-
   Fishing is for me.

   (A Sports for me book)
   SUMMARY: Kevin and his friend Virgil explain the techniques of fishing, equipment, bait, kinds of fish, and preparing fish for cooking.

   1. Fishing—Juvenile literature. 2. Cookery (Fish)—Juvenile literature. [1. Fishing] I. Title. II. Series: Sports for me books.

SH445.T46   1980   799.1′2   80-13442
ISBN 0-8225-1096-0   (lib. bdg.)

Manufactured in the United States of America. Published simultaneously in Canada by J. M. Dent & Sons (Canada) Ltd., Don Mills, Ontario.

International Standard Book Number: 0-8225-1096-0
Library of Congress Catalog Card Number: 80-13442

1 2 3 4 5 6 7 8 9 10 85 84 83 82 81 80

Hello. My name is Kevin and this is my friend Virgil. He's holding up one of the bass we caught this summer. Bass are often large. They can put up a good fight, so it is a great sport to try to catch them. Virgil and I also fish for bluegill. Let me tell you about some of our fishing trips.

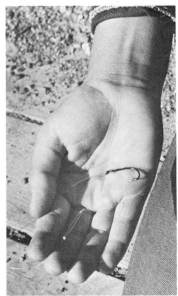

I've been fishing for over a year. When I started fishing, I had only a few pieces of equipment. Fishing equipment is called **tackle**. There is different tackle for different kinds of fishing. My tackle includes a rod and reel, hooks, bobbers, sinkers, a stringer, a net, and a tackle box. Later I'll explain what these items are and how to use them.

One of the most important pieces of tackle is a **rod** and **reel**. The rod is the pole to which the reel is attached. The reel is the piece of equipment that holds the supply of fishing line on the rod. There are many different kinds of rods and reels.

SPINNING ROD AND REEL

SPIN CASTING ROD AND REEL

I use a spin casting rod and reel. My reel is a **closed face** reel. This means the spool on which the line is wound is enclosed in a case. On a spinning, or **open face**, reel, the spool is exposed, or open. But you really don't even need a reel for fishing. A simple bamboo rod with some line attached is also good.

There are many different kinds of water to fish in. Virgil and I fish in lakes and streams because we do not live by an ocean. We go **freshwater** fishing. Ocean fishing is called **saltwater** fishing.

Many people fish for fun, but to me fishing is a serious sport. You must be clever and skillful to catch fish, and you must obey the laws that protect the fish. There are laws that say when you can fish and how many fish you can catch. Most people need a license to fish. In our state, you do not need

a license until you are 16 years old. But this law may be different in your state.

Early mornings and evenings are good times to fish. Many fish feed then, so they will be biting. Virgil and I like to get up early and fish at Hinkley Lake. Dad sometimes drives us over and then joins us in the afternoon.

The first thing Virgil and I do is pick a good fishing spot. We usually fish from the public docks at Hinkley Lake. If you want to fish from someone's property, be sure to ask the owner's permission first.

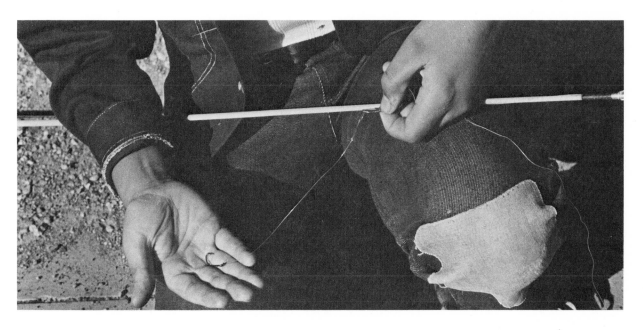

After we pick our spot, Virgil and I get our line ready for fishing. The fishing line on our reels is called **monofilament**, meaning one filament, or one strand. At the end of the line, we attach about 18 inches (45 cm) of **leader**. Leader is a special kind of line that is invisible to fish. Leader is stronger than line, so fish cannot bite through it. The hook is tied on the leader with a knot.

We attach a **bobber** to the line about 36 inches (90 cm) from the hook. A bobber is a small ball that floats on the water. Its bobbing motion will let you know when you've got a bite. When a fish grabs your hook,

the bobber will go under the water. If we are going to fish in deep water, we use **sinkers**. Sinkers are metal weights that are put on the line to hold your hook down in the water.

Virgil and I put live **bait** on our hooks. Bait is anything that you use to catch fish.

We use minnows and worms. We buy the minnows from a store. They must be kept alive in water. We keep the worms alive in some damp soil in a special worm box. If the soil is too wet, the worms will drown. The box should be kept out of the sun or the worms will die from the heat.

Sometimes we get small red worms from my backyard. We turn over the soil to find them. Other times we catch nightcrawlers which are bigger than red worms. You can catch nightcrawlers on your lawn when it is dark outside.

Casting is the way you put the baited hook into deep water. Before you start, you must make sure no one is standing behind you. Fish hooks can be very dangerous. Begin by holding your rod straight out in front of you. The bait will be hanging from the bobber at the tip of your rod. As you lift the rod, keep your thumb on the thumb trigger.

Now move the rod back so that the bait is behind you. With a quick flick of your wrist and arm, flip the tip of the rod forward. As the bait goes out, lift your thumb from the thumb trigger so the line can unreel. As soon as the bait plops into the water, stop the line from unreeling by putting your thumb back on the thumb trigger.

When using live bait, you must cast gently so you don't injure or lose the bait. People who have spent a lot of time fishing can cast very accurately. The bait will enter the water exactly where they aim it.

Hinkley Lake has many different fresh-water fish. I looked in a library book to learn how to identify them. There are bass, bluegills, perch, and catfish. All these fish bite at our live bait, so Virgil and I never know what kind of fish we'll catch.

One morning the fish just weren't biting, and Virgil and I were ready to quit. But just as we were about to move to another location, Virgil's bobber was pulled under the water. He had a bite!

I reeled in my line and got ready to help Virgil.

Virgil raised the tip of his rod firmly, but gently. He did this to **set the hook**, or get it to catch in the fish's mouth. If you do not set the hook, it may slip out of the fish's mouth. If you jerk the rod too hard, you may lose the fish, too.

Virgil took his time **playing the fish**. This means he was letting the fish move about in the water until it tired itself out. Virgil slowly reeled in the line as the pulling of the fish became weaker and the line became loose. It is very important to keep the line **taut**, or tight. If the **tension**, or tightness, becomes too loose the hook may slip free.

I helped Virgil **land** the fish. First, he reeled the fish in close to the dock. Then I slipped a net under the fish and scooped it out of the water. It was a bluegill. A bluegill is in the sunfish family.

Using my thumb and first finger, I removed the hook carefully. Sometimes a fish will swallow the hook. Then the hook is removed with a needle-nosed pliers.

To keep the bluegill fresh, we put it on a **stringer**. A stringer is a cord with a pointed piece of steel at one end. The cord is run through the fish's mouth and out one of its gills. You can stick the steel point into the bank so the fish stays in the water.

Virgil and I caught several more bluegill from the shore that morning. We stopped fishing for a while to eat our lunch. It's so much fun to be out in the country.

After lunch, Dad arrived with our boat.
We would try fishing for bass away from
the shore. Virgil and I helped Dad take the
boat off the top of our car. Then we **launched**,
or put, the boat into Hinkley Lake.

Virgil and I know how to swim, but we still wore life preservers when we went out in the boat.

Dad, Virgil, and I took turns rowing the boat. It sure was easy to go off course!

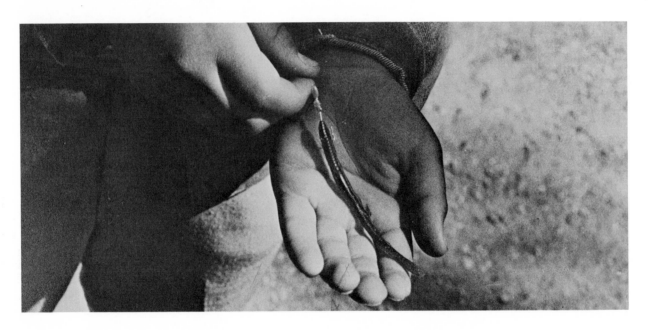

We used a different kind of bait to fish for bass. Instead of live bait, we used artificial bait called **lures**. This lure looks like a fat, juicy nightcrawler. The hook is a part of the lure.

I caught the first bass. It was a large-mouth bass, and it was much bigger than the bluegills we had caught. The bass really put up a fight, but Virgil helped me land it.

Dad, Virgil, and I caught many more fish that afternoon. When we got home, we had to clean them. We eat all the fish we catch.

We cleaned the fish outdoors. My grandfather showed us how to **fillet** (fill·LAY) the bass. To fillet a fish, you remove all the bones and skin from the meat. You need a very sharp knife to fillet a fish.

We did not fillet the bluegill. They were **scaled**. This means the fish's scales were removed.

The fish and fillets were coated with a mixture of cracker crumbs, corn meal, and flour. Then we fried them in oil. Virgil, his brother Arnesto, and I ate until we were full. The fish sure tasted good!

I also go fishing with my grandfather.
He's been fishing ever since he was a boy
and is one of the best fishermen I know.
Grandfather took me on my first trout
fishing trip. Trout are freshwater game fish.
They live in streams and are very hard
to catch.

Grandfather has special tackle for trout fishing. His rod is called a **fly rod**. It is longer and lighter than a regular rod. The lures are called **flies** and look like insects.

We used dry flies that float. The fishing line is special, too. It also floats and is coated to make it waterproof.

Grandfather and I carried his tackle through the woods. As soon as we reached his favorite trout stream, we waded into the water.

Because you stand in the stream when you fish for trout, you should wear boots. I wore special rubber boots called **hip boots**.

Hip boots are high enough to prevent water from going inside and getting your legs and feet wet. Some people wear boots that go all the way up to their chests. These boots are called **waders**.

Trout are smart fish. They stay out of sight and hide in the shadows of trees, rocks, or weeds. My grandfather found a spot that looked promising. There were plenty of places where trout could be hiding.

Casting a fly line takes more skill than other kinds of casting. When fishing for trout, cast **upstream**, or against the current, and let the fly drift **downstream**, or with the current. This makes your bait move like a real insect.

Before casting, **strip**, or pull, about 18 feet (5.4 m) of line from your reel. As you swing your wrist and arm back and forth, let the line out slowly. When all 18 feet are extended and whizzing over your head, send the line over the water and let the fly land.

The first few times I tried fly casting, everything went wrong. Sometimes the line got **snagged**, or caught, in bushes or trees. I had to spend a lot of time working the tangles out of my line. My grandfather said that fly casting takes a lot of practice.

Setting the hook and landing the trout are also difficult skills to master. Trout can put up a terrific fight. You must raise your rod tip over your head and, as you lower it, reel in your line bit by bit.

My grandfather caught two trout that day. They were put into a **creel**. A creel is a wicker basket to hold fish that you catch.

I watched Grandfather clean the trout. Their scales are so tiny you can eat them. Grandfather just washed the fish and removed the insides by cutting a slit down their bellies. Then he cooked the fish whole and cut off their heads right before serving.

Another kind of fishing I want to try is **ice fishing**. My cousin from Minnesota told me about this sport. To ice fish, you drill holes in the ice on frozen lakes or rivers and drop lines into the water. You should only fish on lakes where the ice gets from 8 to 10 inches (20 to 25 cm) thick. Fishing on thinner ice is dangerous.

People who ice fish do not use rods. Instead they use line with special line holders called **jiggle sticks**. There are several different kinds of jiggle sticks, and one kind is a **tip-up**. Because tip-ups hold your line, you do not have to stay right by the holes.

Some people drill several holes. But check the laws before you do this. Some states limit the number of lines you can fish from.

Most tip-ups have a flag that pops up when a fish takes the hook and pulls on the line. When you see the flag, you can go to the hole and land the fish.

Ice fishing really sounds like fun. My cousin's family has a fish house. Every winter they move the house onto the frozen lake and fish from holes in the floor. You can stay much warmer inside a shelter than outside in the cold wind.

My cousin invited me to come to Minnesota next winter during school vacation. He said we can go ice fishing then, and I can hardly wait. Winter seems so far away when it's the middle of summer now.

That's the story of my fishing experiences. I would like to go ocean fishing sometime. It would be exciting to catch some of the larger saltwater fish. My father said we might vacation near the ocean next year. In the meantime, I'll keep fishing the lakes and streams around home. You should try fishing, too!

Words about FISHING

ANGLER: A name for a person who fishes

BAIT: Anything a fish thinks is food, and you are using to catch fish. Bait can be live or artificial.

BOBBER: A small floating object whose motion signals when a fish has taken the bait

CASTING: Sending the bait and hook into the water

CLOSED FACE REEL: A reel with the line enclosed in a metal case; also called **spin casting reel**

CREEL: A wicker basket used to hold fish

FILLET: The meat of the fish that is sliced away from the skeleton and skin

JIGGLE STICK: The piece of tackle that holds your line when you are ice fishing

LANDING: Getting a hooked fish from the water to the shore or the boat. Landing is usually done with a net.

LEADER: A type of fishing line that is almost invisible. Hooks and bait are attached to the leader.

LURE: Artificial bait used to catch fish

MONOFILAMENT: A type of single-strand fishing line

OPEN FACE REEL: A reel on which the line is visible; also called **spinning reel**

PLAYING THE FISH: Reeling a fish in slowly so it becomes tired and does not break your line

REEL: The piece of tackle that holds your supply of line on the rod

ROD: The pole to which the reel is attached

SCALES: The protective covering on the skin of some fish

SETTING THE HOOK: Tugging on the line to secure the hook in the fish's mouth after it has taken the bait

SINKERS: Metal weights that are clipped onto the line to hold your bait down in deep water

SNAG: Getting your line caught on something while you are casting or when your line is under water

STRINGER: A string on which fish are strung and kept in the water

TACKLE: The equipment used for fishing

TIP-UP: A kind of jiggle stick or line holder used in ice fishing

ABOUT THE AUTHOR/PHOTOGRAPHER

ART THOMAS is active in sports as an instructor, a participant, and a fan. As a drama and composition teacher in Cleveland, Ohio, Mr. Thomas is also involved with professional and community theater, both as an actor and a director. In addition, he writes travel and feature articles for newspapers and magazines and has authored other books in the *Sports for Me* series.